FOCUS ON EUROPE

FRANCE
AND THE FRENCH

ANITA GANERI

FRANKLIN WATTS
LONDON • SYDNEY

This edition printed in 2004

© Aladdin Books Ltd 1992

Designed and produced by
Aladdin Books Ltd
28 Percy Street
London W1T 2BZ

First published in
Great Britain in 1992 by
Franklin Watts Ltd
96 Leonard Street
London EC2A 4XD

ISBN 0-7496-5480-5

A CIP catalogue record for this book is
available from the British Library.

Printed in U.A.E.

Designer	Flick Book Design and Graphics
Series Director	Bibby Whittaker
Editors	Jen Green, Suzanne Melia, Fiona Robertson, Mark Jackson
Picture Research	Emma Krikler
Illustrators	David Burroughs Peter Kestevan David Russell Tessa Barwick

The author, Anita Ganeri, has an M.A. in
French, German and Hindi from Cambridge.
She has lived and worked in both France and
Germany and has written numerous children's
books on various topics.

The consultant, Antony Mason, has an M.A. in
French and German from Oxford. He has lived
and worked in France and Germany, and now
writes and edits books for children.

INTRODUCTION

France is a beautiful country, rich in culture and steeped in history. For hundreds of years, its capital, Paris, has been renowned as a world centre of art and learning, and many of the world's most famous writers and artists are French. France is a country of marked geographical contrasts, from the snow-capped Alps to the sunny beaches of the Mediterranean. It is also one of the world's leading agricultural and industrial nations. This book offers an insight into France and the lives of the French people, combining information from the fields of geography, language and literature, science and maths, history and the arts. The key below shows how the subjects are divided up.

Geography

The symbol of the planet Earth shows where geographical facts and activities are included. These sections include a look at the extent of French territory throughout the world.

Language and literature

An open book is the sign for activities which involve language and literature. In these sections, the influence of French literature is examined, and the works of such French writers as Hugo, Molière and Rousseau are discussed.

Science and maths

The microscope symbol indicates where a science project, maths project or science information is included. If the symbol is tinted green, it signals an environmental issue. A look at the perfume industry is included.

History

The sign of the scroll and hourglass shows where historical information is given. These sections look at key figures and events in French history and examine their contribution to society today.

Social history

The symbol of the family indicates where information about social history is given. Descriptions of festivals, holidays, rural and city life combine to create a flavour of France.

Arts, crafts and music

The symbol showing a sheet of music and art tools signals arts, crafts or musical activities. These sections look at French architecture and at the work of French artists.

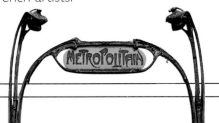

CONTENTS

INFLUENCE AND PRESENCE

France is the largest country in western Europe and one of the most prosperous. It plays a key role in European and world affairs. The influence of French culture, food and fashion has been felt all over the world. The map below shows where the French language is still spoken. Many of these countries were once part of the French Empire, but are now independent. France has a population of about 59 million. It covers an area of about 551,500 square kilometres and includes the island of Corsica and several smaller islands in the Pacific Ocean and the Caribbean.

■ French possessions

1. Guadeloupe
2. Martinique
3. French Guiana
4. St Pierre and Miquelon
5. Réunion
6. Mayotte
7. French Polynesia
8. Wallis and Fortuna
9. New Caledonia
10. Kerguelen Island
11. Crozet
12. Antarctic territories

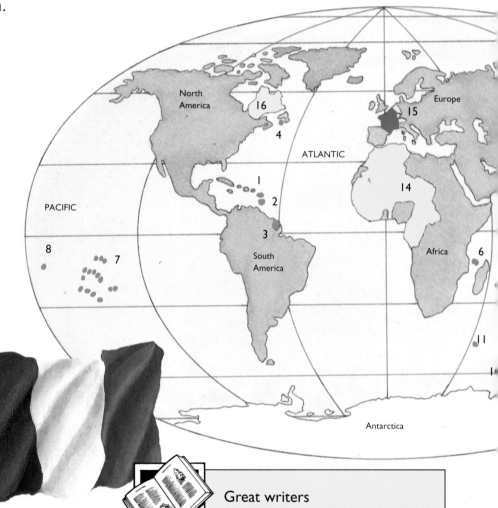

The *Tricolore*

The *Tricolore* (Tricolour) has been the national flag of the Republic of France since 1794. The red and blue represent the city of Paris, and the white is the traditional colour of the French kings. Despite this link with royalty, these colours were adopted during the French Revolution as symbols of freedom (see pages 8/9). *La Marseillaise* has been the national anthem of France since 1795. It was composed by a soldier during the Revolution.

Great writers

France is famous for its writers, artists and composers. Molière wrote comic plays in the 17th century. The writings of the philosopher Rousseau influenced events that led to the French Revolution.

Molière
1622-1673

Jean-Jacques Rousseau
1712-1778

The *fleur-de-lis* (see top left) and the cockerel (below) are famous symbols of France. The kings of France used the *fleur-de-lis* in heraldry. The cockerel represents the fighting spirit of the French.

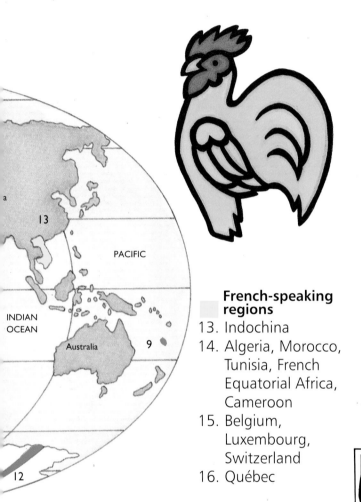

France in the EU

France is a leading member of the EU (European Union). The EU grew out of the European Community (EC), which was set up to establish closer ties in trade, farming, law and politics between the countries of Europe. The EC itself grew out of the European Coal and Steel Community, which France helped to found in 1952. The EU now has 25 member states. The Union can pass laws governing many aspects of life in the member countries. These include areas such as agriculture, the environment, health, food, education, transport and industry. A European Parliament, first elected in 1979, debates all policy issues.

French-speaking regions

13. Indochina
14. Algeria, Morocco, Tunisia, French Equatorial Africa, Cameroon
15. Belgium, Luxembourg, Switzerland
16. Québec

Origins of language

French is a Romance language, derived from Latin. Until the 1500s, however, French was only spoken around Paris. Elsewhere, people spoke regional languages, such as Breton, and dialects. A standardised form of French, called *le bon usage*, was laid down in the 1530s by the writer Rabelais. Further Greek and Latin words were added during the Renaissance (1300-1600), resulting in a beautiful and harmonious language. In 1784, the French author Antoine Rivarol boasted "What is not clear is not French".

French cuisine

French cookery and restaurants are renowned all over the world. The French consider cooking an art. They use only the best ingredients and like to linger over meals. Some of the most famous French delicacies are snails, crêpes, pâté, bouillabaisse (fish stew) and cassoulet (meat and bean casserole). They also consider wine an essential accompaniment to food and may drink more than one variety during a meal.

ORIGINS TO SUN KING

After the collapse of the Roman Empire in the 5th century AD, France was conquered by a Germanic tribe called the Franks. France takes its name from the Franks. They ruled until 895 AD, when Normandy in northern France was settled by Vikings from Scandinavia. They became known as the Normans. Later, it was the English who ruled over large areas of France. They were driven out in the 16th century, leaving the French kings to rule for the next 200 years.

Feudalism

In the Middle Ages (from the 5th to 12th centuries), a system of labour called feudalism was in place in France. Aristocratic lords owned the great estates of land. Peasants, called serfs, worked on the land and paid the lord rent in return for his protection. They had no land of their own and were known as tenants. They had no independence, but the protection of the lord was more important.

French prehistory

Prehistoric people lived in France as long ago as 15,000 BC. Paintings dating from about that time were discovered in 1940 in caves in Lascaux, south-west France. Prehistoric artists had covered the walls with paintings of bulls, bisons, stags, horses and lions. In 1994, hundreds and engravings and charcoal drawings were discovered in the caves of Chauvet-Pont-d'Arc in south-east France. The drawings, which depict mammoths, rhinoceroses and lions, are over 30,000 years old.

Lascaux wall painting

Charlemagne (top left) was the greatest and most powerful king of the Franks. He ruled from 771 to 814 AD. He was a great soldier, fighting over 50 military campaigns. Under his rule, the French Empire expanded to include parts of Spain, Germany and northern Italy. Charlemagne was also a tireless campaigner on behalf of the pope and the Christian Church. In 800 AD, he was crowned Emperor of the Romans by Pope Leo III. After his death, the French Empire was split into three parts.

Charlemagne's Empire in 771

Area added after 771

Joan of Arc

Palace of Versailles

Louis XIV

The Romans in France
Roman armies began to invade France in about 200 B C. Julius Caesar conquered France between 58 and 51 BC and the Romans ruled until 486 AD, when they were defeated by the Frankish king, Clovis. The Romans called France "Gaul". Many Roman remains can still be seen in France, especially in the south. They include bridges, aqueducts and amphitheatres.

Joan of Arc
Joan of Arc (Jeanne d'Arc) was born in 1412. As a young girl, she heard the voice of God telling her to fight the English and restore the French king to the throne. In 1429, Joan led the French army to victory at Orléans. In 1430, however, she was captured by the English and burnt at the stake as a witch. Joan of Arc was made a saint in 1920.

Louis XIV - The Sun King
Louis XIV was nicknamed the "Sun King" because he was thought to be "the sun that lit up France". He ruled from 1643 to 1715, making France the most powerful country in Europe. Louis moved his court to Versailles, outside Paris, where he had a magnificent palace built (above).

REVOLUTION ONWARDS

After Louis XIV died, France went into decline. Ordinary people were poor and hungry. They resented the huge sums of money spent on costly and unsuccessful wars. In 1789, they stormed the Bastille prison in Paris – the French Revolution had begun. The king, Louis XVI, was overthrown and members of the aristocracy were guillotined. France became a republic in 1792. Since this First Republic, France has passed through four other major periods of history (see page 9). Today's France is the Fifth Republic.

The storming of the Bastille 14 July, 1789

The Storming of the Bastille took place on 14 July, 1789. An angry mob attacked and captured the prison. The revolutionaries introduced a charter of human rights, called *The Declaration of the Rights of Man*, and the slogan *Liberté, Egalité, Fraternité*. Bastille Day is still celebrated today in France as a national holiday.

Emperor Napoléon Bonaparte, who built the Arc de Triomphe, below

Napoléon Bonaparte

Napoléon Bonaparte (1769-1821) was a brilliant army general who seized power in 1799. In 1804, he had himself crowned Emperor of France. Napoléon based his empire on that of the Romans, conquering most of Europe and beyond. In 1815, he was defeated by the British at the Battle of Waterloo. Napoléon abdicated and was exiled to the South Atlantic island of St. Helena, where he died in 1821.

Victor Hugo

The poet and writer, Victor Hugo (1802-1885), was a monarchist who became a republican. For this, he was exiled by Napoléon III, but returned to Paris in 1870 where he was regarded as France's leading literary figure. Hugo's two best-known works are the novels *Les Misérables* and *The Hunchback of Notre Dame*.

World War I

France suffered very heavy losses in World War I (1914-1918). Over a million Frenchmen died and around 2 million were injured. The Germans invaded France soon after the war started. For over three years, the border between France and Belgium became the battle front. Some of the worst battles took place around the town of Verdun in north-east France.

Troops in World War I

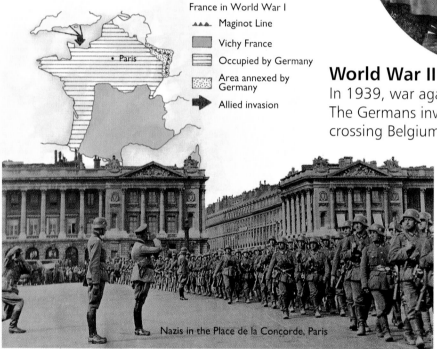

France in World War I
▲▲▲ Maginot Line
Vichy France
Occupied by Germany
Area annexed by Germany
➡ Allied invasion

• Paris

Nazis in the Place de la Concorde, Paris

World War II

In 1939, war again broke out with Germany. The Germans invaded France in 1940, crossing Belgium to bypass the Maginot Line, a series of fortifications thought to be impassable. They occupied about two-thirds of France. Part of southern France remained under the control of the French Vichy Government. In 1942 the Germans took control of the area. France was liberated by the Allies in 1944.

Towards a Fifth Republic

Today's France is called the Fifth Republic. This chart shows the dates of the other four.

1789............. The French Revolution
1792............. France becomes a republic
1804-1815 Reign of Napoléon I
1848............. The Second Republic
1852-1870 Reign of Napoléon III
1871............. The Third Republic
1914-1918 World War I
1939-1945 World War II
1944............. The Fourth Republic
1954-1962 War with Algeria
1959............. Charles De Gaulle establishes the Fifth Republic

De Gaulle

Crisis in Algeria

In the 1800s and early 1900s, the French Empire included many African and Asian colonies. By 1954, some had become independent, but the French refused to let Algeria go. War broke out in Algeria. In 1958, Charles De Gaulle (left), the leader of the Free French in World War II, was elected president, with special powers to tackle the crisis. He organised peace talks which led to a cease-fire in April 1962, and French voters approved Algeria's independence. Algeria became independent on 3 July, 1962, and most French settlers there returned to France.

THE COUNTRY

The countryside of France ranges from fertile farmland around the river valleys to the snow-capped peaks of the Alps and Pyrénées. Mont Blanc, the highest mountain in Europe at 4,807 metres, is part of the French Alps. In the south lies the Côte d'Azur with its sandy beaches; in the centre, the huge block of rugged mountains, called the Massif Central. The climate varies too. It is hotter in the south and west, which benefit from the warming effect of the Gulf Stream current. The Aquitanian Lowlands in the south-west have pine forests, rolling plains and sand dunes. Corsica lies 160 kilometres south-east of the mainland.

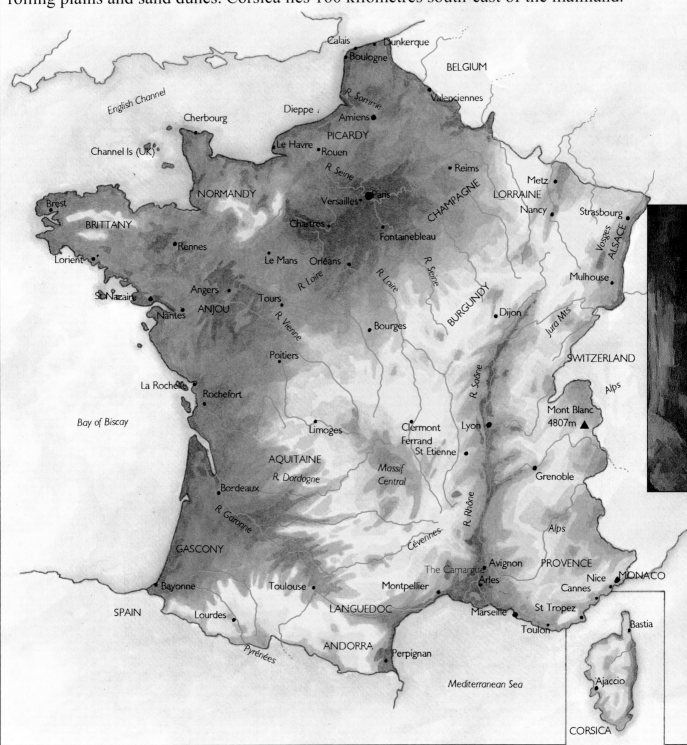

Separate identity

Many of the different groups of peoples in France are keen to preserve their own traditions and identity alongside their French nationality. The Bretons in the north-west have their own dress and language. In the south, the Provençal people also have their own language, which belongs to a group of dialects called Langue d'Oc. The Basques in the south-west and in Spain speak a language called Euskera. On Corsica, most of the population speak a dialect similar to Italian.

Breton dress is still worn by some older Bretons as part of everyday dress.

Savoy Alps costume

Basque costume

Images of landscape

The beauty of the French countryside inspired many of the French Impressionist painters. They tried to reproduce the immediate impression of a scene and the way light appears to the eye. Seurat and Cézanne were post-Impressionists. Cézanne painted Lac d'Annecy (left). He deliberately distorted the natural appearance of his subject to create a more dramatic composition. Seurat used a technique called pointillism (painting with individual dots of pure colour)

in *The Bridge at Courbevoie* (above). Try this technique yourself. Look at your picture from a distance. Do the dots merge to form new colours?

The Camargue

The Camargue is a huge area of marshland in the south of France, where the River Rhône flows into the Mediterranean Sea. It was once famous for its huge herds of black bulls and white horses. The herds are smaller now, but the region is still an important conservation area with a population of over 5,000 pink flamingoes. The Camargue is also the first rice-producing region in Europe - the Rhône's flood plains make perfect rice paddies.

CITIES AND TOWNS

Nearly three-quarters of French people live in cities and towns. Paris is by far the largest city (see pages 14/15). Other major cities include Marseilles, Lyon, Toulouse and Nice. They are centres of trade, industry and tourism. Most French cities are a mixture of old buildings and narrow streets, and modern apartments and offices. Many city centres are now traffic-free zones, with pleasant wide avenues (*boulevards*) and parks to stroll in. Sprawling suburbs have grown up around their outskirts. Public transport systems carry people from the suburbs to a variety of jobs and recreational and cultural activities in the city.

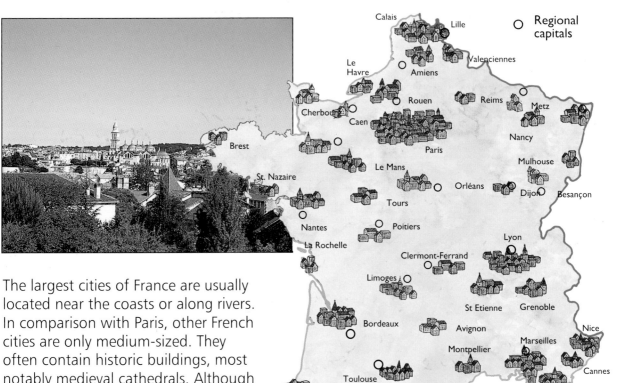

○ Regional capitals

Calais
Lille
Valenciennes
Le Havre
Amiens
Rouen
Reims
Metz
Nancy
Cherbourg
Caen
Paris
Mulhouse
Brest
Le Mans
Orléans
Dijon
Besançon
St. Nazaire
Tours
Nantes
Poitiers
La Rochelle
Lyon
Clermont-Ferrand
Limoges
St Etienne
Grenoble
Bordeaux
Avignon
Nice
Montpellier
Marseilles
Cannes
Toulouse
Biarritz
Toulon
Bastia
Ajaccio

The largest cities of France are usually located near the coasts or along rivers. In comparison with Paris, other French cities are only medium-sized. They often contain historic buildings, most notably medieval cathedrals. Although most French people live in towns and cities, the increase in their populations has recently slowed down.

Working life

Many people live in the city suburbs and commute into the centre each day to work. Over a quarter of France's workforce is employed in manufacturing industries. They work in factories making cars, chemicals, aircraft, machinery and so on. Many also work in service industries, for example, in restaurants and cafés, driving buses or cleaning the streets (right). May 1 is officially celebrated as Workers' Day.

Although the monuments and old buildings of France's towns and cities are well preserved, there are also a lot of new apartment buildings, housing projects and shopping centres. These tend to be located in the suburbs where there is more space and cheaper land. Strict regulations help to protect the centre of many French cities and high-rise constructions may be limited by law.

City living

Pavement cafés are a major feature of life in French towns and cities. They are popular meeting places, where people can eat, drink and chat, or just watch the world go by. There are also museums, art galleries and libraries to visit. Most cities and towns have open-air markets, selling fresh fruit and vegetables. The larger supermarkets, or hypermarkets, tend to be situated on the outskirts of the city.

Traditional architecture

France has much fine, traditional architecture, dating from the Middle Ages (400s to 1500s) to the present day. Gothic cathedrals dominated French architecture from about 1150 to 1300. Chartres cathedral (centre) is a masterpiece of Gothic architecture. Gothic architects developed flying buttresses, which were brick or stone supports built against the outside walls. Ribbed vaults in the ceilings were also a distinctive characteristic.

A more recent French architect, Charles Le Corbusier (1887-1965), led a movement known as the International Style. The major elements of his designs are a geometric shape, white concrete walls, a flat roof and a continuous band of windows.

Rib vault ceiling

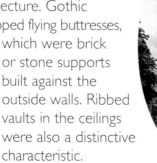

Flying buttress

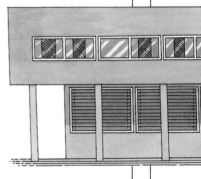

Building by Le Corbusier

PARIS

Paris is France's largest city and its capital. It is the political, industrial and cultural centre of France. It is also one of the most picturesque, and most visited, cities in the world. Paris's world-famous sights include the Eiffel Tower, Montmartre and the Champs-Elysées with its many art galleries and fashion boutiques. There are also many fine hotels, restaurants and theatres. The cathedral of Notre Dame stands on the Ile de la Cité. This is the oldest part of Paris. It is the area where the city was founded about 2,000 years ago by the Romans.

An island in the River Seine, the Ile de la Cité, is the heart of Paris. As the city grew, it soon spread out on both banks of the river. The original city wall has long since disappeared, replaced by the broad, tree-lined *boulevards* built between 1853 and 1870. The River Seine curves through Paris for about thirteen kilometres from east to west, enclosed by high stone embankments and crossed by many bridges.

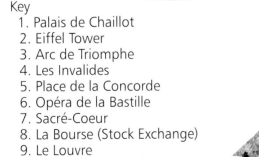

Key
1. Palais de Chaillot
2. Eiffel Tower
3. Arc de Triomphe
4. Les Invalides
5. Place de la Concorde
6. Opéra de la Bastille
7. Sacré-Coeur
8. La Bourse (Stock Exchange)
9. Le Louvre
10. Centre Georges-Pompidou
11. Notre Dame
12. Panthéon
13. Palais du Luxembourg

Modern architecture

In 1989, a modern glass pyramid was built over the entrance to the Louvre, causing huge controversy. One of the biggest and most famous art galleries in the world, the Louvre houses the *Mona Lisa* by Leonardo da Vinci. The sculptured iron entrances to the Métro were also a new style to Parisians in 1900. They are a fine example of Art Nouveau.

Pyramid of the Louvre

Métro entrance

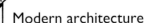

Paris fashion

Paris is one of the main centres of the fashion world. It has been a fashion centre since the 14th century, but the modern fashion industry began in the 19th century. Each spring, designers from all over the world come to view the work of fashion houses such as Yves St Laurent, Chanel and Christian Dior. The Paris collections influence fashion and are copied all over the world.

Art in Montmartre

The white church of the Sacré-Coeur (Sacred Heart) stands on a hill overlooking the district of Montmartre. This was once the haunt of famous artists, such as Toulouse-Lautrec, Renoir and Picasso. The district's music halls, cafés and bars inspired many of Toulouse-Lautrec's paintings. He was also famous for his posters, advertising nightclubs and various other products.

La Défense (below) was opened in 1978. It is a huge complex containing offices, shops, entertainment and sports facilities. Modern sculptures, trees and fountains decorate the complex's pedestrian precinct.

The modern Pompidou Centre (above) was opened in 1977. It contains the National Museum of Modern Art. All its pipes, vents and ducts are on the outside, painted in greens, reds and blues.

Right and Left Banks

The River Seine flows through Paris, dividing the city into the Left Bank and Right Bank. Traditionally, the Right Bank has been the business centre of the city. The Left Bank is where intellectuals, such as the writer and philosopher Jean-Paul Sartre, lived and worked. The Sorbonne (Paris's university) and the student Latin Quarter are on the Left Bank. This area has been called the Latin Quarter since the Middle Ages, when teachers and students spoke in Latin.

Jean-Paul Sartre
1905-1980

RURAL FRANCE

Only about a quarter of French people live in the countryside. The rest live in towns and cities (see pages 12/13). As a result, the French countryside is relatively spacious and uncrowded. It is dotted with farms and villages. Most country people make their living by farming (see pages 22/23). Villages are often very old. The centre point of a village is usually a small square, surrounded by a church, the Mairie (town hall), shops and cafés. This is where people meet to chat or to play *boules* (see pages 20/21).

Once or twice a week, the village has its market day. Markets are often held in the village square. Local farmers come to sell their vegetables, fruit, dairy produce and poultry. There may also be stalls selling clothes, household goods and flowers. The market is a traditional part of French rural life. It is not only a place for shopping, but also for meeting up with friends. Villages and small towns also rely on local shops. Many specialise in one kind of product, like cheese.

Festivals

Many French festivals and holidays are connected to the Church, such as saints' days, Christmas and Easter. There are also smaller village festivals celebrating local produce. These include wine, lavender and cheese festivals, oyster festivals and even nougat festivals. The sign below advertises a festival to celebrate the local agricultural product, in this case pigs. Most villages honour their local patron saints with a festival in July.

Lace-making

Traditional lace is made by plaiting, twisting and knotting strands of linen or silk together by hand. The town of Alençon in Normandy has been a lace-making centre for over 300 years, and still has a lace-making school. Try knotting cord yourself, as below. Tie four loops of different colours over the pins, and follow the diagram. Start by knotting threads A and D together, over B and C. Then H and C, over D and G, and so on.

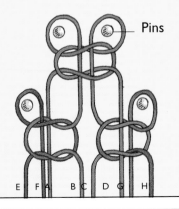

Pins

Religion

The main religion of France is Roman Catholicism. There are churches in every town and village. Over 80% of people are Roman Catholics, more than 5% are Muslims (mainly from North Africa) and about 2% are Protestants. From 1801-1905 the Church was linked to the state. Priests were state officials, paid by the government. This church is a typical example of those found in most small towns.

Market day is a busy and exciting day in most French towns. The streets and cafés are crowded.

The châteaux

There are *châteaux* all over France. Some are small manor houses; others are magnificent palaces which once belonged to the kings and aristocracy. The most famous *châteaux* are those in the Loire Valley. Many date from the Renaissance period in the 16th century. The best examples include those at Fontainebleau, Chambord and Azay-le-Rideau. Many *châteaux* have their own vineyards and are famous for their wine production.

Château de Lavauguyon (below) is situated in the district of Haute-Vienne. It is a fine example of impressive Renaissance architecture.

The Château Prieuré-Lichine (left) is a small, wine-producing manor house in the Médoc region.

ORGANISATION

France is a republic (*La République Française*) with a democratically elected government. The president is head of state and is elected for five years at a time. The president can serve an unlimited number of terms and appoints the prime minister. The prime minister, or premier, is head of the government and chooses who will serve on the cabinet (the Council of Ministers). Parliament is made up of two houses. The National Assembly has over 500 members, called deputies. The Senate has over 300 members, called senators.

The offices and official residences of the president, prime minister and the various government bodies are all in Paris. They are located in many historic and impressive buildings, as follows:
President - Palais de l'Elysée
Prime Minister - Hôtel Matignon
Seat of Parliament - Chambre des Deputés
National Assembly - Palais Bourbon
Senate - Palais du Luxembourg
Supreme Administrative Court - Palais Royal

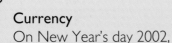

Currency
On New Year's day 2002, France, along with eleven other member countries of the EU, introduced the euro as their unit of currency. The euro replaced the franc, however, many features of the old franc now appear on french euro coins. For example, a tree symbolizing life, continuity and growth is encircled by the motto *Liberté, Egalité, Fraternité*.

The president of France lives in the Palais de l'Elysée (top), built in 1718. The main house of parliament, the National Assembly, meets in the Palais Bourbon, above, completed in 1728. The National Assembly is more powerful than the Senate and makes the final decision.

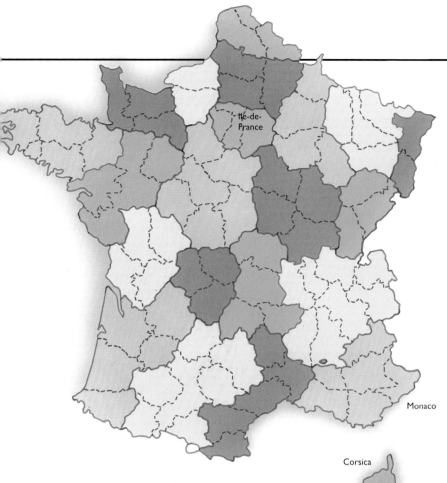

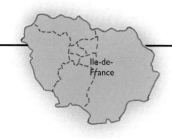

Ile-de-France

Monaco

Corsica

Départements

France is divided into 22 local government regions. These are further divided into 96 areas, called *départements*. Each *département* has its own number which is used as a postcode and on car registration plates. Each *département* has a commissioner who reports to the national government in Paris. Each of the 22 regions has a regional council, elected by the people, and a president elected by the council members. The Paris region is divided into eight *départements*, known as the *Ile-de-France*. The smallest unit of local government is the *commune,* which ranges in size from villages to cities.

The Palais du Luxembourg (above) is the meeting place of the Senate. The palace was built during the early 1600s. The Palais Royal (right) is the meeting place of the Supreme Administrative Court.

The legal system
The French legal system is based on the system used by the Romans. The highest court in the land is the Court of Cassation. It can hear appeals from the regional criminal and civil courts, and has the power to review cases and overturn decisions. The Court of Assizes hears cases of murder and other serious crimes. French judges are appointed by the Minister of Justice. They hold their positions for life. The French police force is known as *La Police* and the policemen are called *les agents de police.* *Gendarmes* (top left) belong to a branch of the French military.

EDUCATION AND LEISURE

Education is very important in France, but so is sport and leisure. Sports, such as football, cycling, tennis, horse racing and rugby, are followed very closely. French people have about five weeks holiday per year. Many head to the mountains for skiing, or to the coasts where they like to sail, swim and windsurf. They also enjoy going to cafés and restaurants, and to the cinema and theatre.

The annual *Tour de France* is one of the most important sporting events in France. Over a hundred top-class cyclists take part in the race, which lasts for 26 days. The cyclists cover about 4,800 kilometres of France. The race finishes in Paris.

From the ages of 2 to 6, many children go to nursery school. From 6 to 11, they attend primary school. They go to a *collège* from the age of 11 to 15. Then they go to a general *lycée* to study for the *baccalauréat* examination, or to a vocational *lycée* to train for a job. If students pass the *"bac"*, they can go to university. There are 89 universities in France, together with the more élite Grandes Ecoles.

Boules

Boules, or *pétanque*, is the national game of France. It can be played in any flat, open space, such as a village square or a park track. It is a similar game to bowls. The winner is the player whose boule is closest to the jack.

1. The first player (red) draws a circle to stand in and throws the *cochonnet* (jack) about 6.5 to 10 metres forward.

2. Then she throws her first boule as close to the jack as possible. She must remain inside the circle as she throws.

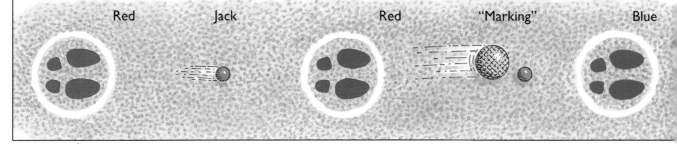

Red   Jack   Red   "Marking"   Blue

Gérard Depardieu

The theatre and cinema are very popular with French people. Famous names of French cinema include Juliette Binoche and Gérard Depardieu. Each year, in April and May, the International Film Festival is held in Cannes in south-eastern France. Actors, actresses and film-makers from all over the world go there to promote their latest films. The *Comédie Française* in Paris is the most famous theatre in France. It was established in 1680 by King Louis XIV. It is the state theatre of France and all the best plays are performed there.

3. The second player (blue) stands in the circle and tries to throw his boule closer to the jack.

4. The person furthest away (red) can try to knock the other boule out of play or get their boule nearer to the jack.

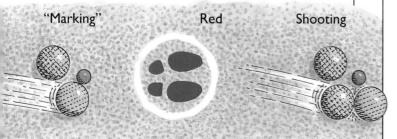

"Marking"   Red   Shooting

Braille

Braille is a system of writing and printing for blind people. It was invented by Louis Braille (1809-1852). He had been blinded in an accident at the age of three. The Braille system uses six raised points, used in over 60 combinations. Blind people read Braille by running their fingers along the dots.

Louis Braille

All for one...

As well as adult literature, French authors are world famous for their children's writing. Alexandre Dumas (1802-1870) wrote his best-known novel, *The Three Musketeers*, in 1844. Jules Verne wrote *Around the World in Eighty Days* (1873). Charles Perrault (1628-1703) is best known for a book of fairy tales. Published in 1697, *Tales of Mother Goose* included *Sleeping Beauty*, *Puss in Boots* and *Cinderella*.

Astérix is a popular character amongst children and adults. The adventures of *Astérix the Gaul*, by Goscinny and Uderzo, have been translated into every major language.

AGRICULTURE AND FOOD

Agriculture is very important in France. Over half of the land is used for farming. Food and farm goods make up about a fifth of France's exports. Farmers raise animals, such as beef and dairy cattle, sheep, poultry and pigs. Fish and seafood are caught along the west coast and the Mediterranean. Among the main crops grown are wheat and other cereal crops, fruit, such as grapes and apples, and sugar beet. France produces about a quarter of the world's wine – only Italy produces more. France also produces some 400 varieties of cheese, many of which are world famous.

Many regions and towns in France are known throughout the world for their wine, cheese, mustard and so on. The map below shows just a small selection of famous French foods.

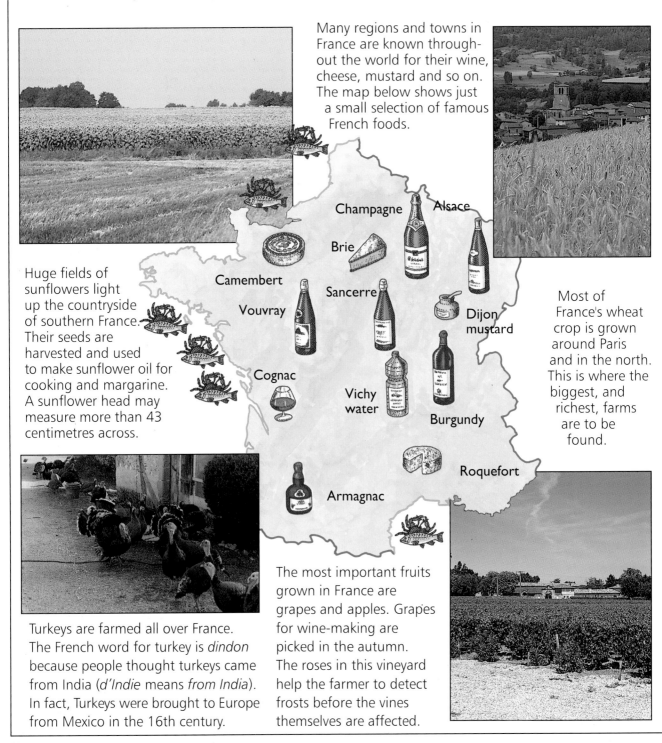

Huge fields of sunflowers light up the countryside of southern France. Their seeds are harvested and used to make sunflower oil for cooking and margarine. A sunflower head may measure more than 43 centimetres across.

Most of France's wheat crop is grown around Paris and in the north. This is where the biggest, and richest, farms are to be found.

Turkeys are farmed all over France. The French word for turkey is *dindon* because people thought turkeys came from India (*d'Indie* means *from India*). In fact, Turkeys were brought to Europe from Mexico in the 16th century.

The most important fruits grown in France are grapes and apples. Grapes for wine-making are picked in the autumn. The roses in this vineyard help the farmer to detect frosts before the vines themselves are affected.

Wine-making

To make white wine, white and red grapes are crushed (1), then pumped into a press (2). The juice goes into a vat to ferment (3). It is fermented completely to make dry wine (6), half fermented for sweet wine (4) or bottled early to make sparkling wine (5). The dry wine may be distilled (7) to make brandy (8). To make red wine, red grapes are crushed (9) and fermented in a vat, usually with their skins (12). Some wine is drawn off after about a fortnight (13). It is then pressed and squeezed (15) with the skins (14). Rosé (17) is made in the same way, but drawn from the vat (12) earlier and put in a second vat to ferment (16). Fortified wines (18) are made from trodden red grapes (10). The juice is fermented (11), then mixed with brandy from the still (7).

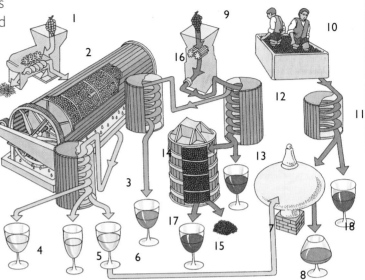

Louis Pasteur

Louis Pasteur (1822-1895) was a chemist and biologist. He found that diseases are spread by bacteria (germs). Pasteur also found that bacteria could turn milk and beer sour. He developed a process, now known as pasteurisation, which uses heat to kill the bacteria. It is still used today to make milk safe. Pasteur became director of the Pasteur Institute in Paris (see page 29).

A la carte

A French restaurant is an ideal place to learn about French food and practise your French. Here are some words to help you with the menu:

la carte - menu
le couvert - place setting
les hors d'oeuvres - starter
le potage - soup
le poisson - fish
la viande - meat
les pommes frites - chips
le pain - bread

le beurre - butter
les légumes - vegetables
le fromage - cheese
la glace - ice cream
la crêpe - pancake
le café au lait - white coffee
le vin rouge - red wine
le vin blanc - white wine

Bon appétit! Enjoy your meal!

Making a crêpe

To make a thin, French pancake, or crêpe, sift 65 grams of plain flour and a pinch of salt into a bowl. Add an egg, 3 tablespoons of milk and one of oil. Mix the batter well. Leave it for an hour, then pour a little into a hot frying pan.

INDUSTRY AND EXPORT

France is one of the world's leading industrial countries. A programme of modernisation began in the 1950s. As a result, France now has important iron and steel, car and chemical industries. It is in the top five of world exporters and sells its goods to almost every country. France is at the forefront of technology and engineering. It has an excellent transport system, boasting the TGV (*Train à Grande Vitesse*), below centre. This is the world's fastest passenger train, with average speeds of over 210 km/h. The smart car (below) is one of the strongest, safest and most environmentally-friendly small cars ever made.

Citroën

France is the world's fourth largest producer of cars. Only Japan, the U.S. and Germany make more. French cars, such as Citroën, Renault and Peugeot, are world famous. The car-making factories are mainly found around Paris, Lyon and Rennes. They use most of the metal produced by France's iron and steel industry. The badges of the top three car manufacturers are shown here.

Peugeot

Renault is the largest of the three. France has a large network of roads. You have to pay a toll to drive on the motorways, or *autoroutes*. Many people prefer the smaller *routes nationales,* or "N" roads.

Renault

The smart car, part of DaimlerChrysler group, is assembled in France's Alsace-Lorraine region in a factory complex called "Smartville".

The perfume industry
Some of the finest, most famous, and most expensive types of perfume are French. They include Chanel, Worth and Dior. Perfume has been a major industry in France since the 1920s, although it has been made there since the 16th century. Flowers, such as lavender (right), are grown in the south. Their fragrance (called essential oil) is extracted to make delicate and costly scents. Grasse is where most French perfume is made.

Limoges porcelain

The town of Limoges, on the River Vienne, has been making fine porcelain since the 18th century. The industry had originally established itself in Sèvres during the 1750s, under the patronage of Louis XV. By the 1800s, however, Limoges had taken over as one of the largest porcelain centres in Europe. The impressionist painter, Renoir (1841-1919), worked for a time as a porcelain painter in Limoges.

Sabatier knives

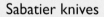

Sabatier is a name chefs all over the world would recognise. For over a hundred years, Sabatier has produced fine quality knives from French steel (see page 26). First established in 1885, Sabatier boast that their knives are forged from a single piece of steel. Next time you visit a kitchen shop, look out for the symbol of the lion and the label "Made in France".

Those magnificent men

The French aircraft industry has been a pioneer in air travel. In 1793, the Montgolfier brothers made the first ever flight in a hot-air balloon. In 1874, Felix du Temple designed the first successful powered plane (pictured right). In 1903, the American Wright brothers made the first controlled and manned powered flight in their plane, *Flyer I*. This inspired the first flight in Europe, made in France by a Brazilian, Alberto Santos-Dumont in 1906. In 1909, Frenchman Louis Blériot made the first flight across the Channel. By the 1970s, France was manufacturing the Airbus A300 series (photo left), and today, the all-new superjumbo A380 is assembled in Toulouse.

Du Temple
1874

Santos-Dumont 14BIS
1906

Blériot XI
1909

Concorde, the world's first supersonic passenger plane, first flew in 1969. It was a joint venture between the British and French. However, it is now out of service, having made its last flight on October 24, 2003.

The Concorde 1969

RESURCES

To keep its industries running, France needs large amounts of raw materials. It has some natural resources (below) and it imports others, such as minerals and chemicals. Forests cover about a quarter of France, making timber a major natural resource. Yet, France does not have huge supplies of oil and gas. To supply energy to its factories, homes and schools, it has turned to alternative forms of energy (bottom and below right), and invests huge amounts into the research of new energy sources such as nuclear power. The French have used their resources to complete huge feats of building, such as the Channel Tunnel, which now links France and England.

Mining resources
France has large supplies of coal, iron ore and bauxite. It also has some oil, gas and other minerals. These are mined and used in industry. Iron ore is particularly important for making steel for the car industry. The largest supplies of iron ore are found in the Lorraine area in the north-east. Bauxite (aluminium ore) is found in the south-east. It gets its name from the town of Les Baux. Aluminium is a light metal used to make drinks cans and cooking foil.

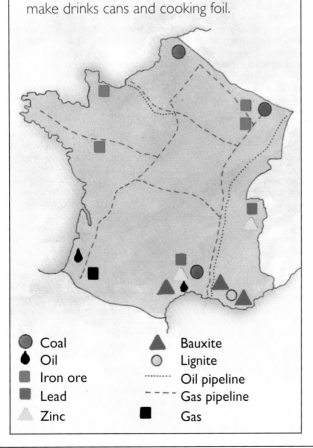

⬤	Coal	▲	Bauxite
⬥	Oil	◯	Lignite
◼	Iron ore	⋯⋯	Oil pipeline
◼	Lead	---	Gas pipeline
▲	Zinc	◼	Gas

Tidal power
The world's first tidal power station was built in 1966 at the mouth of the River Rance in Brittany. It extracts energy from the rising and falling of the tides. These tides can be extremely high, sometimes reaching a height of 13 metres. The energy in the water turns devices called turbines, which are used to generate electricity. The French have also built a solar power plant at Odeillo in the Pyrénées. The sun's rays are concentrated using mirrors and are then used to heat water. The steam given off drives turbines. This is how the sun's energy is used to make electricity.

Marie Curie

Marie Curie (1867-1934) and her husband, Pierre Curie (1859-1906), are famous for their study of radioactivity and their discovery of the radioactive elements, radium and polonium. Marie also studied uranium, the main nuclear fuel. In 1903, they won the Nobel Prize for physics. In 1911, Marie won a second Nobel Prize, for chemistry, for her work in isolating radium. She also helped found the Radium Institute in Paris in 1914.

The Channel Tunnel was opened in the mid-1990s. It consists of three tunnels – two rail tunnels and a service tunnel. Eurostar trains (left) carry passengers and *Le Shuttle* transports cars and goods under the sea between Folkestone, England, and Calais, France.

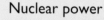

Nuclear power

Over a third of France's electricity comes from nuclear energy and is produced in power stations like the one below. The rest comes from oil, gas or coal, or from hydroelectric power stations, located in the Alps and Jura mountains. France is a world leader in nuclear research. Aiming for self-sufficiency, France produces its own nuclear fuels. It has one of the best safety records in the world. The French government consider it a clean and efficient source of energy and have invested huge sums in establishing new plants.

TODAY AND TOMORROW

France continues to have a great influence on the rest of the world through its art and culture, trade, language, scientific research and its political ties. It is proud of its independent spirit, but also works closely with other countries in Europe and the rest of the world. France does suffer from some social problems, such as unemployment. But it also enjoys a high standard of living and is a world leader in agriculture and industry. Its mixture of traditional and modern has made it a very popular place to visit. The France of the future will continue to play a major part in world and European affairs, whilst remaining a proud and independent country.

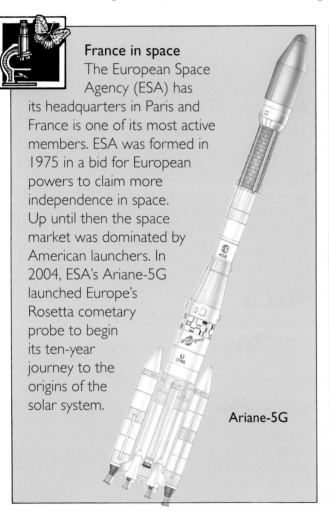

France in space
The European Space Agency (ESA) has its headquarters in Paris and France is one of its most active members. ESA was formed in 1975 in a bid for European powers to claim more independence in space. Up until then the space market was dominated by American launchers. In 2004, ESA's Ariane-5G launched Europe's Rosetta cometary probe to begin its ten-year journey to the origins of the solar system.

Ariane-5G

Flag of United Nations

France and the UN
France is a leading member of the United Nations (UN). This international organisation was set up after World War II to maintain peace and security and solve the social and economic problems faced by its members. Since France joined the UN in 1945, its troops have been part of peace-keeping forces around the world, most recently in Africa, the Middle East and the Balkans. Paris is the headquarters of UNESCO (the United Nations Educational, Scientific and Cultural Organisation).

The European Parliament
Strasbourg, in north-east France, is the seat of the European Parliament. It meets to debate EU policies put forward by the Council of Ministers.

Flag of the European Parliament

The French foreign legion
The French foreign legion is an army of fearsome volunteers, mainly from countries outside France. It was formed by King Louis Philippe in 1831. French-men are forbidden to join the Legion but some enlist by giving false nationalities. At the end of their period of enlistment, legionnaires are entitled to French nationality.

Médecins sans frontières

Médecins sans frontières (Doctors without frontiers) is a French charity which seeks to bring medical care to trouble-hit areas of the world. Its officials often risk their lives or risk being taken hostage to work in places such as the Middle East and Africa.

NATO

NATO

NATO (North Atlantic Treaty Organisation) was established in 1950. France signed the North Atlantic Treaty in 1949 with 11 other nations. The treaty stated that an armed attack against a member state in Europe or North America would be considered an attack against all members. Differences between France and the United States led to the withdrawal of French forces from NATO in 1966, however, they rejoined NATO military command in 1993. NATO's headquarters are in Brussels, Belgium.

ESA

The European Space Agency promotes the development of a space programme in Europe (see page 28).

Tourism

France is one of the world's most popular tourist destinations. It has sandy beaches, mountains, forests and picturesque towns and villages. The French Alps attract thousands of people every year to ski resorts such as Chamonix and Val d'Isere. In 1992, the Euro Disney resort opened in Marne-la-Vallée, about 30 kilometres outside Paris. One of its main attractions is Sleeping Beauty's castle (*Le château de la Belle au bois dormant*). The resort covers an area one fifth the size of Paris, and employs thousands of people from all over the world.

AIDS research

France is at the forefront of present, and future, research into the disease AIDS. AIDS attacks the body's immune system and often results in death. The first AIDS virus was identified in 1983 by a team of French researchers, led by Dr Luc Montagnier of the Pasteur Institute in Paris. New cures for AIDS are being tested all the time, but research continues.

France is a country that embraces the future, whilst preserving the treasures of the past. French people now enjoy a standard of living that is higher than ever before, yet still strive to maintain their traditions and a culture that has succeeded in touching every corner of the world.

FACTS AND FIGURES

Name: La République Française (The French Republic)

Capital and largest city: Paris (population: 9.5 million)

National motto: Liberté, Egalité, Fraternité ("Liberty, Equality, Fraternity")

National anthem: *La Marseillaise*

Official language: French

Population: 58,886,000

Population density: 106 people per sq km

Currency: As of 2002 the euro, previously the franc.

Life expectancy: 78 years

Distribution: 74% live in urban areas, 26% live in rural areas.

Ethnic groups: French 93.5%, Portuguese 1%, Algerian 1%, Moroccan 1%, Italian 0.5%, Spanish 0.5%, Turkish 0.5%, other 2%.

Religion: Roman Catholic 76%, Muslim 5.5%, Protestant 2.5%, Jewish 1%, other (including unaffiliated) 15%.

Area: 551,500 sq km

Size: Maximum east-west: 974km; north-south: 950km

Highest mountain: Mont Blanc 4,807m (in the Alps)

Largest lake: Lac du Bourget, east of Lyon, 43 sq km

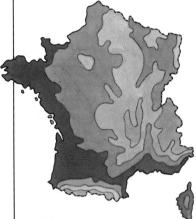

Celsius

Above 4
2-4
0 to 2
Below 0

AVERAGE JANUARY TEMPERATURES

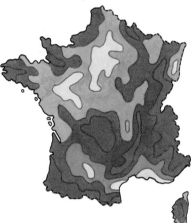

Centimetres

More than 100
80-100
60-80
Less than 60

AVERAGE ANNUAL RAINFALL

Celsius

Above 22
20-22
18-20
Below 18

AVERAGE JULY TEMPERATURES

Longest rivers: Loire, 1,010km; Rhône, 810km; Seine, 770km; Garonne, 650km

Climate: Summer – warm, winter – cool. On the Mediterranean coast, all the seasons are warmer (see climate maps above).

Location/physical features: On the western edge of Europe. Much of north-central, northern and western France has either rolling hills or is flat.

Coastlines: on the Atlantic Ocean, Mediterranean Sea and English Channel.

Borders: with Belgium, Luxembourg, Germany, Switzerland, Italy and Spain.

Mountains: Pyrénées (forming the Spanish border), Alps (forming the Swiss and Italian borders), Juras (forming the Swiss border), Massif Central (in south-central France).

AGRICULTURE

Crop production 2003: (tonnes) Wheat 30.7 million, sugar beet 29.3 million, corn (maize) 11 million, barley 10 million, grapes 7 million, potatoes 6.4 million, rapeseed 3.3 million, dry peas 1.6 million.

Land use: Arable 33%, forests and woodland 27%, permanent pastures 20%, permanent crops 2%, other 18%.

INDUSTRY

The following are just some of the leading industries in France's industrial sectors: construction and civil engineering; agri-food stuffs; chemicals, rubber and plastics; pharmaceuticals; automobile industry (below); metallurgy; metal processing; telecommunications and postal services; shipbuilding; aerospace; railway locomotives.

Imports

Machinery and transport equipment 38%, agricultural products 11%, chemicals 8%, fuels 7%.

Major import sources:

Germany 18%, Italy 10%, UK 9%, Belgium/Luxembourg 9%, Spain 6%, U.S. 6%.

Exports

Machinery and transport equipment 43%, agricultural products 15%, chemicals 8%, plastics 3%.

Major export destinations:

Germany 18%, Italy 9%, Belgium/Luxembourg 9%, U.K. 8%, U.S. 7%.

Tourism

France is the world's most popular tourist destination with some 67 million foreign tourists visiting France every year. France has some 17.3 million tourist beds, 16.1 million of which are in rural gîtes, camp sites and youth hostels. As a result, France generates a trade surplus of some 11 billion U.S. dollars.

ELECTRICITY

Production by source:

Nuclear	76%
Hydroelectric	12.5%
Fossil fuels	11%
Other	0.5%

ECONOMY

The GDP (gross domestic product) is the amount of goods and services produced within a country. By dividing the GDP by the population a *per capita* result is reached.

Figures shown are the GDP per capita in the year 2002 (GDPs are shown in U.S. dollars).

France	25,767
U.S.	35,935
Belgium	28,964
Germany	26,234
U.K.	25,427
Italy	24,915
Spain	20,660

France is the world's fourth largest car producer, building some 3.6 million vehicles each year.

FAMOUS FACES

LITERATURE

Molière (1622-1673). See page 4.

Jean Racine (1639-99). Born near Meaux. One of the greatest French playwrights. Wrote during the French Classical Age. The essence of his work is simplicity, with limited dialogue and little action.

Victor Marie Hugo (1802-1885, left). Born in Besançon. Led the Romantic movement in French literature. His writings reveal his love of liberty and sympathy with ordinary people. Lived in exile from 1855 to 1870.

Gustave Flaubert (1821-1880, right). Born in Rouen. Master of the realistic novel, perpetually sought "le mot juste". *Madame Bovary* (1856) is considered the most perfect French novel.

Emile Zola (1840-1902). Made naturalism the leading form of French literature in the late 1800s. Novels include *Thérèse Raquin* (1867) and *Germinal* (1885). Zola's major novels are rich in symbolism.

Marcel Proust (1871-1922). Born in Paris, his most famous work is *A la Recherche du Temps Perdu*. Work on Baudelaire and Flaubert shows him to be a sensitive critic also.

André Breton (1896-1966). Poet, author, playwright and performer. Originally a member of the dada group, which rejected authority and challenged conventional artistic ideas. Breton abandoned dada to become the leading figure of the Surrealist movement, probably the single most influential artistic force last century. His work includes *Nadja* (1928) and *Soluble Fish* (1924).

Jean-Paul Sartre (1905-1980). See page 15.

Simone de Beauvoir (1908-1986, left). Born in Paris, she was an author and philosopher. Ideas she shared with Sartre were later called "existentialism". Famous works include *The Second Sex* (1949) and *Memoirs of a Dutiful Daughter* (1958).

ARTISTS

Nicholas Poussin (1594-1665). Poussin thought painting should appeal to the mind, not the senses. Most of his subjects were biblical or mythological. He was First Painter to Louis XIV, King of France.

Edouard Manet (1832-1883, right). Born in Paris. Often associated with the Impressionist style, Manet's work is renowned for its rich colours and textures. Most famous painting is *Bar at the Folies Bergère*.

Edgar Degas (1834-1917). Degas was a post-Impressionist painter and sculptor.

Paul Cézanne (1839-1906). See page 11.

Claude Monet (1840-1926). Born in Paris, he was a leader of the Impressionist movement. Especially concerned with the effect of outdoor light and atmosphere, he painted several series of pictures showing the effect of sunlight on a subject.

Auguste Rodin (1840-1917). Born in Paris. One of the greatest sculptors of the 1800s, he was influenced by Michelangelo. Created human figures with great emotional intensity.

Pierre Auguste Renoir (1841-1919, left). Born in Limoges. An impressionist painter, famous for his pictures of young girls and children, and for his scenes of cheerful middle-class life.

Paul Gauguin (1848-1903). Born in Paris. Style deliberately distorted nature by enclosing broad, flat areas of colour with heavy contours. His pictures idealised the peoples of the South Sea islands as gentle and passive.

Georges Seurat (1859-1891) developed a system of painting called Pointillism. This method used lots of dots of bright colour side by side, instead of brushstrokes.

Henri de Toulouse-Lautrec (1864-1901). See page 15.

Henri Matisse (1869-1954, right). Born near Cambrai. A highly influential artist of the 1900s. Matisse was leader of the Fauves, one of the most important art movements of the era. Also a noted sculptor, book illustrator and tapestry designer.

MUSICIANS

Georges Bizet (1838-1875, left). Born Paris. Wrote *Carmen*, the most popular opera of all time. Was a brilliant pianist, although his main interest was in composing, especially operas. His music is very melodic, with a relatively simple orchestral arrangement.

Gabriel Urbain Fauré (1845-1924, right). Born near Toulouse. Composer of songs and song cycles (series of songs). Style characterised by an extensive use of harmony. Most famous works include *Requiem* (1900), *La Bonne Chanson* (1894) and *La Chanson d'Eve* (1906-10).

Claude Debussy (1862-1918, left). Born in St-Germain-en-Laye. Greatly influenced by language and literature in his work. Was the leader of Impressionism in music, and his radical style helped to change the direction of music in the early 1900s.

Maurice Ravel (1875-1937). Born in Ciboure, near the Spanish border. Spanish influence can be heard in his work. Most popular composition is the ballet music *Bolero* (1928).

SCIENTISTS

René Descartes (1596-1650, below left). Philosopher, mathematician and scientist. He invented analytic geometry and was a pioneer in formulating simple, universal laws of motion. Coined the phrase "I think therefore I am".

Blaise Pascal (1623-1662). Born in Clermont-Ferrand, he was a physicist, mathematician and philosopher. His work on the pressure of fluids produced the principle "Pascal's law".

Antoine Laurent Lavoisier (1743-1794). Born in Paris, he was the founder of modern chemistry. He studied combustion and discovered and named oxygen. Lavoisier published his findings in his *Elementary Treatise on Chemistry* (1798).

Baron Cuvier (1769-1832). A naturalist who pioneered the founding of palaeontology (the study of fossils). He wrote a book on zoology, *The Animal Kingdom*.

Louis Jacques Mandé Daguerre (1787-1851). Introduced the first popular form of photography. His pictures were called daguerreotypes.

Louis Braille (1809-1852). See page 2.

Louis Pasteur (1822-1895). See page 23.

Marie Curie (1867-1934). See page 27.

Louis Blériot (1872-1936, left). See page 25.

Jacques-Yves Cousteau (1910-1997, right). Cousteau was an oceanographer, author and film producer. In 1943, helped invent the aqualung. Has explored the oceans in his research ship *Calypso* and promoted conservation of the seas and oceans.

ENCORE! ...

Clovis I (466?-511). A Frankish king who defeated the last great Roman army in Gaul (now called France).

Joan of Arc (1412?-1431). See pages 6/7.

Louis XIV (1638-1715). See page 7.

Marie Antoinette (1755-1793). Born in Vienna, she became queen of France after marrying Louis XIV and died on the guillotine during the French Revolution. She became unpopular with the people due to her frivolities. Is best known for her phrase "Then let them eat cake", in response to the Parisians' anger at having no bread.

Maximilien de Robespierre (1758-1794, left) was the most famous and controversial leader of the French Revolution (see page 8). He was the chief instigator of the Reign of Terror in 1793 which led to the execution of thousands of his opponents. His extremism made him unpopular and he was guillotined himself.

Napoléon I (1769-1821). See page 8.

Charles De Gaulle (1890-1970). Born in Lille, he became the outstanding French patriot, soldier and statesman of the 1900s. Led the French resistance in World War II and guided the formation of the Fifth Republic in 1958. President for 11 years.

Francois-Maurice Mitterrand (1916-1995, right). Born in Jarnac, near Cognac. Elected president of France in 1981 and 1988. The first socialist president since 1958.

French words used in English

adieu	goodbye
à la mode	fashionable
à propos	by the way
au fait	familiar with
avant-garde	ahead of its time
beau monde	fashionable society
bête noir	a person or thing that is especially disliked
carte blanche	to be given absolute power or authority
cause célèbre	a cause that arouses public feeling
c'est la vie	that's life
comme il faut	as it should be
coup de grâce	the final blow
crème de la crème	the best
cri de coeur	heartfelt cry or appeal
crime passionel	a crime of passion
de rigueur	required by etiquette
déjà vu	a sense of having seen something before
entente cordiale	a friendly understanding between two nations
en masse	in a large group or body
entre nous	between ourselves
fait accompli	an irreversible fact
faux pas	a social blunder
haute couture	high fashion
je ne sais quoi	a distinct and mysterious quality
jeu d'esprit	witty comment
joie de vivre	love of life
laissez-faire	to leave alone
mot juste	the exact expression
nouveau riche	ostentatious from newly acquired wealth
par excellence	to the highest degree
passé	old fashioned
pièce de résistance	highlight of an occasion
raison d'être	reason for being
risqué	indelicate or suggestive
sang-froid	calm self-control in the face of difficulty
savoir-faire	to know how to act appropriately
tête-à-tête	an intimate conversation
tour de force	an outstanding feat
vis-à-vis	relative to, compared with
voilà	there you have it
volte-face	an about turn

INDEX

Photocredits

Abbreviations: l-left, r-right, b-bottom, t-top, c-centre, m-middle

Front cover, back cover, 1, 2, 5b, 7b, 8, 12-13, 13br, 14t, 14m, 15tr, 16 all, 17 all, 18br, 20t, 22t, 22ml, 22bl, 22br, 24t, 24c, 25t, 26t, 28t, 29br — Select Psictures. Front cover inset — Digital Stock. 5t, 11b, 12t, 12bl, 12r, 15b, 18t, 24br, 27l — Spectrum Colour Library. 6, 9b, 14b, 19t, 19b, 20bl, 20r, 21t, 21l, 21b, 24mr, 27r, 29t, 29m, 29bl — Frank Spooner. 7t, 13bl, 15tl, 28-29 — Eye Ubiquitous. 9t — Hulton Deutsch. 9m, 13t, 21tr, 28b — Mary Evans Picture Library. 10, 22mr — Angela Graham. 18m — Robert Harding. 18bl — PBD. 23, 24bl, 25b — Roger Vlitos. 26m — Owen Franken/CORBIS. 31 — Scania.